YOU CAN DO IT

GUIDE TO GREAT SCHOOL REPORTS

by Leslie Lauderdale

illustrated by Estella Hickman

Dedicated to
Marianna Miller Lauderdale
and
Janice Smith Payne

Published by Willowisp Press, Inc.
401 E. Wilson Bridge Road, Worthington, Ohio 43085

Printed in the United States of America

10 9 8 7 6 5 4 3 2 1

ISBN 0-87406-350-7

The author gratefully acknowledges the kind assistance of two super teachers from a super school: Ann Myers and Bob Kellogg from Olde Sawmill Elementary School, Dublin, Ohio.

Thanks also to their students who shared their comments and experiences:

Leah Allen
Joshua Bitter
Karrie Brandt
Micki Brooker
Leigh Brookes
Jennifer Brown
James Clark
Shanna Clark
Adam Cooley
Becky Crabb
Lori Davito
Doug DeVore
Eric Dixon
Brent Dyke
Julie Ferrara

Nathaniel Filler
Robin Freund
Michelle Greek
Tisha Hawley
Steve Helmrich
Corey Holben
Jason Holdridge
Rashad Khan
Michael Lennertz
Stephen Martinez
Matt Mazeika
Leslie McDaniel
Jennifer Minter
John Palguta
Gina Panico

Leslie Regalia
Katie Robinson
Tammy Ruzicska
Mike Schreiber
Mike Schultz
Tom Shelley
Craig Scythes
Rachel Slaybaugh
Greg Snyder
Chad Thomas
Sean Van Pelt
Michael Walters
Kacy Whalen
Carrie Williams
Amy Wood
Marlene Zipin

CONTENTS

1

Getting a good start on great school reports

Wouldn't it be neat if great written reports flew out of your pen the minute you put the pen on paper? Just think how much time and energy you would save if you could skip the research and invent a paper out of your head!

What Do You Mean, "Report"?

"Report," "school report," "written report," "paper," "research paper," or "term paper," are all names for the process of researching a topic, studying the information, and then writing a paper that uses the information in an organized and clear way.

Dream on. Any teacher alive can tell when you've spent 15 minutes in the rest room frantically writing some half-baked report on "The Mysteries of Jupiter."

But with a little effort and planning you *can* make your dream paper a reality. You can do it! Researching a topic and then writing a paper isn't some mysterious process.

There are eight major steps to writing a school report. If you take it one step at a time, trying your hardest, you will end up with a great school report.

EIGHT STEPS TO WRITING SUCCESS

1 **Choose a topic.** Selecting a subject that will meet with your teacher's approval is your first task. In this step you need to take a "big idea" and turn it into a great topic.

2 **Do some preliminary research.** Do some research before you have made a final decision on your topic. You need to find out how many reference sources are available. This will also help you "fine-tune" your idea into a strong topic choice.

3 **Find your resources.** Your next step is to locate the reference material that you will use to write your paper. It can be found in books, magazine articles, or other resources such as videotapes or interviews with people. Writing a bibliography at this point will keep your information organized.

4 **Gather information.** Read your reference material with understanding and take careful notes. The information that you gather at this stage becomes the body of your paper.

5 **Write a topic sentence.** The topic sentence describes the main idea of your paper. It will become the first line of your report. A good topic sentence will help direct you as you write the outline and the body of your paper.

6 **Make an outline.** You outline your report to help organize the information that you have gathered. Outlining puts this information into a logical order.

7 **Write the rough draft.** After all the research and organization is done, you can finally begin writing your paper. The first version of your report is called a "rough draft." It is "rough" because it may contain mistakes in grammar, spelling, punctuation, or structure. Who cares? The rough draft is your first try at getting all the information together in a written form.

8 **Revise to produce a final draft.** Your last step is to polish your rough draft into a final version that shows off all the basics of good grammar and composition.

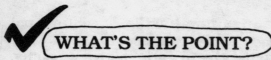

WHAT'S THE POINT?

School reports are written for a purpose. Your teacher may assign a specific purpose for your paper. It may be *to inform* ("Sleeping Habits of Sixth Graders in Mr. Miller's Science Class"), *to persuade* ("Disney World Is the Greatest Vacation Spot in the Universe"), or *to instruct* ("How to Build a Skateboard Ramp").

While the information that you gather and the paper you write using it are important, they aren't the entire point of your assignment. Your teacher is looking for these three things:

☐ **Research skills.** By learning to use resources such as the card catalog and reference books, you are improving your research skills. The ability to locate information when you need it will be important to you throughout your schooling and even when you become an adult.

□ **Organizational skills.** Organizational skills are what you use to build your information into a completed paper. Arranging your note cards in a logical order, outlining your paper into specific steps, and writing a paper that clearly says what you want it to say are examples of these skills.

□ **Writing skills.** Using proper grammar and punctuation is only a part of writing well. Good reports should show thought and creativity as well as the basic standards of good composition.

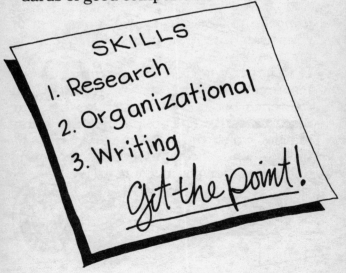

SKILLS

1. Research
2. Organizational
3. Writing

Get the point!

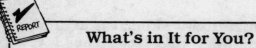

What's in It for You?

Knowing how to research, organize, and write aren't just abilities you will need for your school papers. You can use these skills right now in a lot of ways. Some examples are:

Writing for the school newspaper.

Researching a science fair project.

Organizing a project to earn a Scout badge.

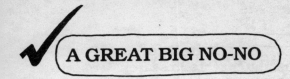

A GREAT BIG NO-NO

When you are facing a project as big as a school report, you need to have a plan to get everything done in the right order at the right time. Putting off starting your paper may seem like a good idea now, but it won't feel that way the night before your paper is due.

Writing a paper is like eating a big meal. You could gobble it all down and get it over quickly, but you would end up feeling sick. When you eat too fast, everything winds up tasting like brussels sprouts. You may get that same sick feeling from doing a hurried job on your report.

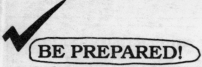

BE PREPARED!

Before you start researching and writing your paper, take a few moments to plan what the paper should include and to put together a schedule for getting everything done.

Your teacher will give you some specific guidelines for your report. Each teacher may have a slightly different idea about how a paper should be done, but, regardless, your job is to *do exactly what your teacher asks.* If she wants the paper typed, find a typewriter. If he wants it written in blue ink, put away your black pen. Following the instructions is just as important to your overall grade as the content of the paper.

The Teacher-Pleasing Paper Planner shown here includes some of the items that your teacher might require for your paper. There may be others which you can also include on the form. Make a copy of it and take some time now to fill it out as completely as possible. Once you have written your paper, come back to this page to make sure that you have followed every instruction carefully.

Teacher-Pleasing Paper Planner

Topic _____

Date Final Draft Is Due _____

  Section Due Dates:

    Topic Approval _____

    Note Cards_____

    Outline _____

    First Draft _____

Presentation Requirements

  Handwritten_____Typed _____

  If handwritten, what
    color ink? _____

  How many pages in length? _____

  Single-spaced?__   Double-spaced?__

  How wide should margins be? _____

  How many research resources are
    required? _____

  What information goes on the cover
    or title page? _____
    _____

  Have you included the appropriate
    supporting items?

    Maps _____ Charts _____

    Graphs _____ Pictures _____

  Should the paper be in a folder or
    notebook? _____

2

Choosing a topic: Hatch an idea!

Which came first, the chicken or the egg? It's a dumb-sounding question, but think about how it applies to writing a report. Before you start writing your paper you have to hatch an idea that can grow into a topic.

If your teacher has given a *specific* topic assignment to you, such as "Inventions That Changed the World," you can skip this chapter for now.

Often teachers assign a more *general* topic, saying something like, "Write a paper about the American Revolution." In this case you will have to think of your topic in more detail. If you're facing such a task, skip to the section titled "Now Think Smaller!" It's a little further on in this chapter.

If your teacher gives you complete freedom in selecting a topic for your report, you need to begin to "think big"!

✓ THINK BIG!

When you can pick almost any subject for your report, the best thing to do first is "think big." Don't worry about the small details of your paper yet. You will have plenty of time to "fine-tune" your idea later. For now, spend some time thinking about ideas that might start you on the way to an interesting report. If you think that you'd like to write about plant life, don't worry yet that you don't know exactly what your paper will say. At least you've eliminated animals and minerals!

WHAT DO YOU KNOW?

Sharing information that you already know and learning about something that has always interested you are two likely ways to come up with a topic.

You probably have lots of interests that you could develop into a report. Your hobbies or experiences have taught you things you could share with others. Stamp collecting, skateboarding, or collecting baseball cards all could be the basis of an interesting report. Soccer, lacrosse, or hockey could make interesting subjects as well.

If you have always been interested in learning a little more about some subject, this is a great time to dig right in. Have you ever wondered how compact disc players work? Would you like to be a fashion model? Do you think you would like to try hang gliding?

Researching your paper will give you answers to such questions, and you might even end up with a new hobby.

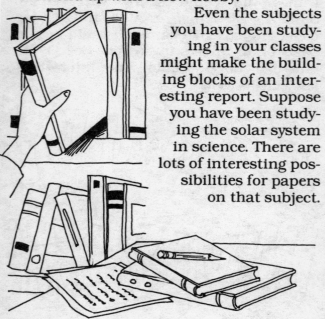

Even the subjects you have been studying in your classes might make the building blocks of an interesting report. Suppose you have been studying the solar system in science. There are lots of interesting possibilities for papers on that subject.

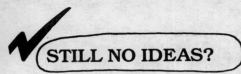

STILL NO IDEAS?

If you are still having trouble thinking of a topic, try skimming through an almanac or encyclopedia for an idea. Or just walk through the nonfiction section of the library and pick up a book at random. There are hundreds of interesting ideas within the covers of a book such as *The Book of Lists* or *Information Please Almanac.*

Finally, somehow, some way, you come up with a subject for your report. It seems like a miracle!

NARROWING THE FOCUS

NOW THINK SMALLER!

So far you've been thinking of your topic in broad terms. Before you start writing your paper you must narrow your topic to a workable size.

When you use a camera, you *focus* on a certain point to get a clearer picture. *Narrowing the focus* of your paper means looking in more detail at a smaller part of your topic.

Some topics are so big that you would need to write a book to cover one of them completely. Since your assignment is to write a report, you need to think smaller.

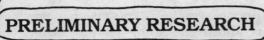

PRELIMINARY RESEARCH

The best way to identify the smaller subjects that make up your bigger topic is to do some preliminary research. Preliminary research means surveying broad information about your topic at the beginning of the research process.

Begin your preliminary research with a general reference book, such as an encyclopedia. Your teacher will frown on using encyclopedias as the only resource for your paper. Keep her happy—use them, instead, as a starting point.

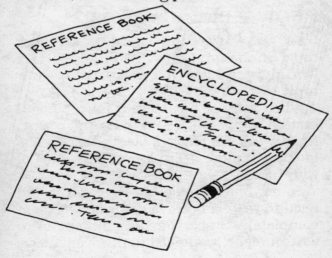

Suppose you've decided to write a report about the solar system. When you look up "solar system" in an encyclopedia, you find a short article with paragraphs about astronomy, early astronomers, planets, meteors, comets, asteroids, space travel, and astronauts. Any of these would make a good topic!

At the end of the encyclopedia entry, sometimes there are notes that direct you to other related subjects. Find those encyclopedia entries and scan them. By now you should have a better idea of what you want to write about.

Breaking It Down

Sometimes when you are writing a paper, you can break the topic down into related subjects. For a report called "Heavenly Bodies," you could write about meteors, asteroids, and comets. Don't try to cover more than three things in this type of paper or it will become too difficult to handle. Remember that all the items should have something in common.

Other papers could be:

"Danger under the Sea" (killer whales, sharks, and sting rays)

"Marsupials" (kangaroos, koala bears, and wombats)

"American Mountain Ranges" (Sierras, Appalachians, and Rocky Mountains)

Can you think of other subjects for a report that you could break down into parts? Try it.

✓ LOOK BEFORE YOU LEAP

When you are narrowing the focus of your paper, you have to be careful not to make the topic *too* narrow. Trying to write a report about a tiny idea could be as hard as writing about a huge idea.

If your teacher expects a 15-page report, he won't be happy with a 5-page or a 30-page report.

There are several problems that you might face as you define the topic for your school report.

☐ **Will your teacher go for it?** Don't kid yourself about the importance of this step. Your teacher expects certain standards in your paper. She will probably have to approve your topic before you begin your research. Suggesting a report on "Why Fourth Graders Are Nerds" or "The 15 Rudest Noises You Can Make with Your Mouth" isn't going to score any points with your teacher. Besides, she has to read the finished paper, and you don't want your topic to make her sick. Think of how it will affect your grade!

DO YOU HAVE THE TIME?

☐ **Do you have the time?** Time is important in planning your paper. You must follow specific steps in the writing process, and each step must be in order. Spending too much time on one step will get you off schedule and make it difficult to do a good job. When you choose a topic, then, it should be one that can be researched easily in the time available.

☐ **Are there resources?** Have you chosen a topic that is too current for many references to be available? Your teacher may require as many as 10 sources for your report. If you can't come up with enough references, you may find yourself in trouble. Subjects that might fall into the "too new" category include recent scientific discoveries, high-tech products, or current events.

Narrow the Focus

MY TOPIC IS . . .			
Way too broad	Still too broad	Just right	Too narrow
Sea Animals	Whales	How Whales Communicate with Song	Whale Songs to Sing in the Shower
Birds	Penguins	Sleeping Habits of Penguins	What to Wear to a Penguin Pajama Party
California	Archaeology in California	Prehistoric Findings in the La Brea Tar Pits	Things I've Found under My Bed in California
Pets	Dogs	Crime Busters: Dogs That Sniff out Drugs	Famous Dog Collars

THE NAME GAME

PUT PURPOSE IN YOUR TITLE

TITLE

You don't name a baby until you know whether it is a boy or a girl. But with a school report you need to come up with a title *before* you start writing so you will know what you are creating.

Including the purpose of your paper in the title will help remind you of the direction you should take. If the purpose of your report is to instruct, you might want to use a "how-to" title, such as "How to Start a Stamp Collection." If you are writing a persuasive paper, you could include, "why" in the title, such as "Why Indoor Soccer Is More Fun than Outdoor Soccer."

Titling your paper before you start will help you do the actual writing in these ways:

☐ **The title shows boundaries.** When you narrow the focus of your paper, you decide exactly what you will cover and what you won't cover. Showing this in your title will be helpful to you when you continue your research. If your paper is titled "Halley's Comet," you don't need to look up general articles about the solar system or about other comets.

☐ **Keeps you from getting lost.** A solid title will keep you from getting lost in a sea of research, note cards, and loose ends. If you keep your mind on your title, you should be able to stay on the subject.

Once you have come to a clear idea of your subject by doing some preliminary research and narrowing the focus, you are ready to start on the next step in the writing process: finding resources.

3

Finding resources: The search begins!

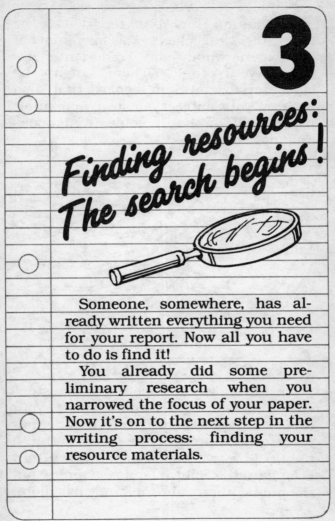

Someone, somewhere, has already written everything you need for your report. Now all you have to do is find it!

You already did some preliminary research when you narrowed the focus of your paper. Now it's on to the next step in the writing process: finding your resource materials.

Information for your report can be found in lots of places. You may know of an expert whom you could interview about your topic. There might be videotapes or museum displays that shed light on your subject. Most of your information will probably come from books and magazines.

✔ NEXT STOP: THE LIBRARY

The library is the place to do "one-stop" searching for information about your topic. Everything you need for your research can probably be found within a public library. Your school library may even have the right reference sources, but the public library almost surely has more.

It's time to head to the library. When you walk in, find your way to the reference section, walk right up to the reference librarian, and introduce yourself. Tell her who you are and what you are writing about. Then ask for guidance in beginning your search.

This may seem like a weird thing to do, especially if you have used the library before and are starting to get familiar with the materials. It's not all that strange, though. Reference librarians are specially trained to use all the information sources in the library. Even if you think you know what books to use for your research, a short chat with the reference librarian could save you lots of time and some false starts.

The two most important sources of information for your paper will be books and magazines. Two special resources will help you locate this type of information. The reference librarian will introduce you to the card catalog and to the *Reader's Guide to Periodical Literature*.

☐ **Card catalog.** The card catalog is a file containing information on all the books within the library. Cards are classified by subject, author's name, and title. Each card contains information about a book and where it is located within the library. Many libraries now have computers instead of file cards. The computerized card catalogs contain the same information as the old cards but in a different order.

Use the card catalog to look up your subject. There is a card for every book in the library.

Let's look at a card catalog file so you can see how to find your books.

523.6   Halley's Comet

A83g   Asimov, Isaac, 1920-
           (Guide to halley's comet)

        Asimov's guide to halley's
        comet/Isaac Asimov.
        New York: Walker, 1985

                [118] p. :illus.

This card on Halley's Comet is for a book titled *Asimov's Guide to Halley's Comet.* The book was published in New York by Walker in 1985. It is 118 pages long and has illustrations.

An important piece of information is the call number of the book. You use this number to locate this particular book on the library shelves.

□ **The *Reader's Guide to Periodical Literature*.** The *Reader's Guide to Periodical Literature* is an index to magazine articles. The entries are listed both by author and by subject.

A new index is published annually, and sometimes supplements are also available. You might need to look in more than one volume to find articles about your topic.

Here is an example of a listing from the *Reader's Guide to Periodical Literature*:

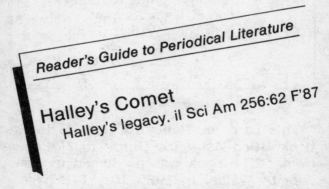

Reader's Guide to Periodical Literature

Halley's Comet
Halley's legacy. il Sci Am 256:62 F'87

This magazine article is titled "Halley's Legacy." It is an illustrated article that appeared in volume 256 of *Scientific American*, on page 62. The article was in the February 1987 edition.

The reference librarian will help you find any back issues of magazines you need for your report.

The Children's Magazine Guide

Some libraries carry a reference source called the *Children's Magazine Guide.* This is a monthly subject index to articles published in children's magazines, such as *Highlights, Children's Digest,* or *Ranger Rick.* Children's magazines have lots of illustrations, and the articles are short. If your library has this reference source, try using it to locate an article for your report.

41

☐ **Other sources.** There are several other likely sources for information on your report. The reference librarian maintains a special collection of material called a *vertical file*. Vertical files contain a hodgepodge of items relating to your subject. These files might contain newspaper clippings, booklets, posters, or teacher's materials about the subject.

The library might also have filmstrips or videotapes that contain useful information about your subject.

THREE EASY STEPS

✔ (A TEST YOU'LL LOVE!)

Now that you have found a pile of books and magazine articles about your subject, what do you do with them? Relax. You don't have to read every word of every page. There is a quick test you can use to find out how useful each book will be for your research. Take the test *before* you lug home 50 pounds of books. Avoid the drag of a dead end by testing your books before you begin your research.

This test has three easy steps:

1 **Skim the table of contents.** First look at the table of contents for a few moments. Is there an entire chapter devoted to your subject? Is there no mention at all of your subject? Glancing at the contents page will give you a general idea of the focus of the book. If you are still wondering whether this book will be useful, take the next step.

2 **Skim the index.** The index will show every page number that mentions your specific topic. Are there a lot of entries? Or does your topic have only a few index entries? A quick look at the index should give you a solid clue to how much material the book includes on the topic. If you want to be sure that the material is valuable to your research, take the next step.

3 **Skim the referenced pages.** The last step in the test is to skim through some of the pages that were listed in the index. Try to grasp the author's main idea quickly. Think about the focus of your paper and decide whether this book will be useful to you.

How did the book score? If you think it made the grade, use it for your research.

GIVING THE EXPERTS CREDIT

Once you locate information sources, you need to start keeping a *bibliography*. A bibliography is a listing of all the sources you use to write your report. A bibliography is almost always required for a report.

Bibliographies show that you have researched your facts and can prove that they are accurate. They are also a way of giving credit to the person who did the original research. By giving authors' names, you can show that experts have been the source of your information.

You will do your bibliography in two phases—bibliography cards and the bibliography page.

BIBLIOGRAPHY CARDS

Bibliography cards are kept on 3 x 5-inch or 4 x 6-inch index cards. These cards are the earliest stage of your bibliography page. The cards will make it easier to weed out the books you don't actually use and to help in alphabetizing your final bibliography page.

Each reference source is written on a separate index card. The cards are easy to handle and should contain the same information as your later bibliography page.

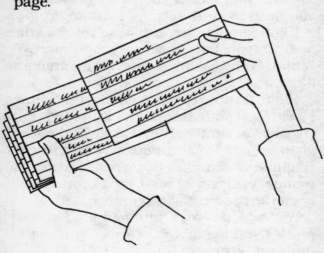

Pick a Number

Here's a neat trick! Number each of your bibliography cards in the upper right hand corner. When you begin taking notes, you won't need to write the title of your books again and again—just write down the card number!

Use a different format for your entries, depending on whether they are encyclopedias, books, magazine articles, or personal interviews. These rules generally apply to all types of sources:

1. Book titles and magazine names are underlined.
2. Each item on the bibliography is separated by a comma.
3. The second and all following lines are indented.

(Your teacher might tell you a different way to do this. Be sure to ask your teacher if there is a specific format he would like you to use.)

ENCYCLOPEDIA ARTICLE IN A BIBLIOGRAPHY

Encyclopedia entries are usually in this order:

1. Article title
2. Encyclopedia name
3. Publication date

"Halley's Comet," *World Book Encyclopedia*, 1988 edition.

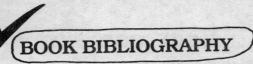

BOOK BIBLIOGRAPHY

Book entries show information in this order:

1. Author's last name
2. Author's first name
3. Book title
4. Publisher
5. Publication date

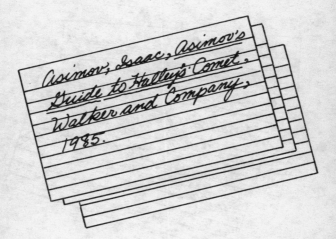

Asimov, Isaac. *Asimov's Guide to Halley's Comet.* Walker and Company, 1985.

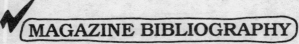

MAGAZINE BIBLIOGRAPHY

A bibliography entry for a magazine article is done in this order:

1. Author's last name (if given)
2. Author's first name (if given)
3. Title of article
4. Name of magazine
5. Date of publication
6. Beginning page number of article

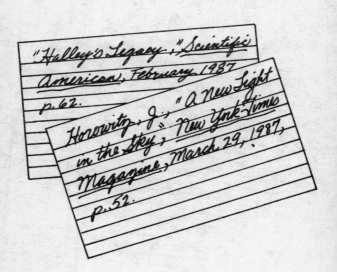

"Halley's Legacy," *Scientific American,* February 1987 p. 62.

Horowitz, J., "A New Light in the Sky," *New York Times Magazine,* March 29, 1987, p. 52.

PERSONAL INTERVIEW BIBLIOGRAPHY

If you interview someone for your research, you will need to give that person credit in your bibliography. Here is one good way to order this type of entry:

1. Last name of person interviewed
2. First name of person interviewed
3. Name of person doing the interview
4. Date of interview

Notice that the two names are separated by a period instead of a comma.

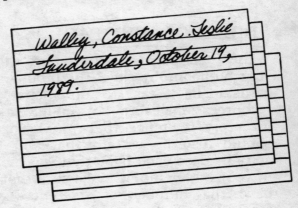

Walley, Constance. Leslie Lauderdale, October 14, 1989.

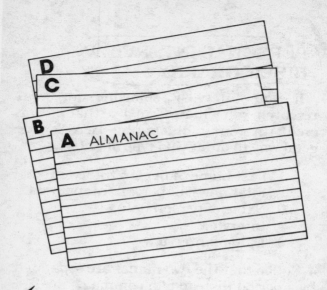

✓ BIBLIOGRAPHY PAGE

The final page of your report will be your bibliography page. The bibliography cards make it easy to alphabetize your resources. Make sure that you have a card for every reference that you used. You should also be certain that you have actually used each book that you include in your bibliography. Make sure that you have the number of references your teacher requires.

Bibliography

Asimov, Isaac, Asimov's Guide to Halley's Comet, Walker, 1985.

"Comet," World Book Encyclopedia, 1988 edition.

Flaste, Richard, New York Times Guide to the Return of Halley's Comet, Times Books, 1985.

"Halley's Comet," World Book Encyclopedia, 1988 edition.

"Halley's Legacy," Scientific American, February 1987, p. 62.

Tattersfield, Donald, Halley's Comet, Basil Blackwell, 1985.

"Visitor From Outer Space," Life, January 1987, p. 98.

Walley, Constance. Leslie Sauderdale, October 19, 1989.

✔ OFF TO A GREAT START!

Now that you have used the library to gather your resource material and have written your bibliography, you are off to a great start. It is time to get down to the business of taking notes and organizing your research into a written report.

4

Take note!

Taking good notes for your report gives you a chance to think about what you've read and to translate the information into your own words. Taking notes doesn't mean that you can copy word-for-word from reference books. Writing something in your own handwriting doesn't make the information your own.

Most of what you will read for your report will contain information that is not necessary or useful to your paper. Taking notes will help you select the information you can use. Good notes will also help you organize and understand the information that supports your topic.

Note-taking does three important jobs:

1

Records factual information. Take notes of factual information that supports your topic. You need to write this information down so that you won't forget it. If you try to carry it in your head, you may end up with a big jumble of loose ends and missing information.

2   **Uses your own words.** Don't be tempted to copy down somebody else's words and try to pass them off as your own. You aren't fooling anyone, but you *are* missing an important part of your assignment.

When you take notes, you should summarize what you read by writing it down in your own words. This is called *paraphrasing*. You will also want to *condense* the information. This means to write down only the most important words and phrases. Condensing and paraphrasing will help you weed out things that don't apply to your topic.

How to Paraphrase and Condense

"When Europeans emigrated to North America, they did not distinguish between the harbor porpoise and the Atlantic bottle-nosed dolphin, *tursiops truncatus*, which is the common inshore toothed whale on the eastern coast of North America. Consequently, the Atlantic bottle-nosed dolphin also became known as porpoise, and the name still finds common usage and scientific acceptability, although technically it is incorrect."

This information about the porpoise uses a lot of long words. You might condense and paraphrase its meaning like this:

American immigrants didn't know the difference between the harbor porpoise and the bottle-nosed dolphin. They thought they were both porpoises. People still confuse them. "Porpoises," Collier's Encyclopedia, 1975 edition.

When you paraphrase and condense, you don't have to use complete sentences. But make sure that you can clearly understand the idea when you go back to your notes.

3 **Records quotes.** Sometimes a book or article says something that you feel you must include exactly as it was written. This is a *direct quotation* from your source. Using quotations can be tricky. Your teacher won't want you to use too many in your report (and some teachers won't like them at all). Choose quotations carefully and make sure that they support your topic better than your own words would. Always put quotation marks around a direct quote.

"The Navy Cross was created in 1919 for 'extraordinary heroism in connection with military operations against an armed enemy.'" —The Children's Encyclopedia, p. 64.

✓ KEEPING NOTE CARDS

One good way to take notes is to use index cards, as you did for your bibliography. They are flexible and easy to use. You will be arranging and rearranging the order of your notes many times. Using note cards makes organizing your outline and report easier.

Here are some rules to follow:

□ **Include only one type of information on each card.** If you write several notes on a card, you won't be able to rearrange your notes easily. Cards are cheap!

□ **Write on one side of the card.** You'll drive yourself crazy if you have to keep turning your cards over to find missing notes. Write on one side only so you will be able to spread your cards all out in front of you. Be sure to leave some space at the top of each card. You'll need this space to write a subject heading at the top when you begin arranging your cards.

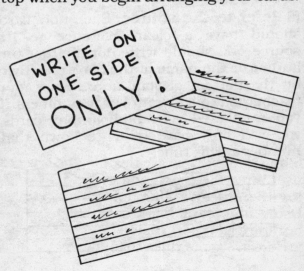

☐ **Write clearly.** You will probably start taking notes in your neatest handwriting. After a few cards, your hand will get tired, your brain will get tired, and your handwriting will *look* tired. Make sure that your handwriting is readable. Use abbreviations only if you will be certain what they mean when you look at your cards next week. Take your time.

Write Clearly!

☐ **Refer to the source.** Each note card should have a clear reference to its source. You should write down either the author or the name of the book or article on the bottom of your note cards. Your teacher may also require page numbers. If you numbered your bibliography cards, you will only have to write down that number at this time.

Encyclopedia
p. 104

✓ TOPIC SENTENCES

At some point in your note-taking, you will begin to get a glimpse of what your final paper will say. Writing a topic sentence will help you define your paper by stating that main idea. Every report must include a topic sentence at its beginning.

When you review your note cards you will begin to see that the information is falling into a pattern. Your topic sentence answers the question "What is my paper about?"

It does it in this way:

☐ **It is a statement.** Your topic sentence clearly states the main idea in a declarative statement. It never asks a question; it supplies the answers.

TOPIC SENTENCE = ONE IDEA!

☐ **It contains only one idea.** Don't try to explain all the details of your report in the first sentence. Make this statement general. It should state the single topic that is covered by your report.

☐ **It is specific.** Be clear. A good topic sentence will help direct your paper. Keep your report on track with a clear topic sentence.

☐ **It is not a personal response.** Your report isn't about you. Don't write a topic sentence that shows how you feel about the information.

Topic Sentences

It's Not a Personal Matter!

Don't do this:

I think volcanoes are very interesting.

Do this:

Volcanoes are openings in the earth that shoot out lava, gases, and rocks.

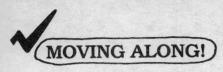

MOVING ALONG!

Once you've taken your notes on note cards and boiled that information down into a solid topic sentence, you are ready to begin your report outline.

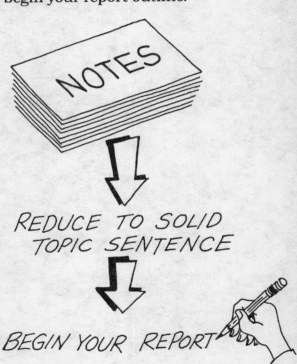

NOTES

REDUCE TO SOLID
TOPIC SENTENCE

BEGIN YOUR REPORT

5

Outlining: The bare bones

An outline is the skeleton of your paper. You create the "bare bones" from your general headings and more detailed sub-headings. When you actually write your report, you add the flesh that makes it complete. Outlining will help you see the connections between your points.

Writing a good outline is a very important step in the writing process. Your teacher will probably want to approve your outline before you begin writing your report. It is not a step that can be skipped.

The outline strengthens your final report in several ways:

☐ **Organizes information.** You've been collecting all sorts of information for your report. A written outline will help you form your piles of note cards into a structure. Your notes will begin to fit together like the pieces of a puzzle.

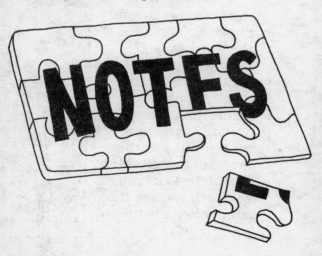

☐ **Points out gaps in information.** Writing an outline will make it clear where your information is sketchy. You may think that you understand where your paper is heading. Until you put together an outline, though, you can't be sure that you have the facts needed to take you where you want to go. You may discover that you need to do more research.

☐ **Keeps you on track.** A good outline is the map that you will use to write your report. Follow it from point to point to arrive at your finished report. An outline has no unnecessary details to lead you off track.

☐ **Helps decide the order of information.** When you write an outline you make decisions about the order in which you will present your information. You might have to try several different outlines before you end up with the one you like.

All of these advantages add up to the greatest help that your outline provides you—it saves lots of time when you actually begin writing your report.

NOTE CARDS TO THE RESCUE!

The way to start writing your outline is to take your stack of note cards and spread them out. Read them again to get an idea of all the information you have gathered.

✓ GROUPING YOUR CARDS

Your next step is to separate the cards into groups of related notes. It's sometimes hard to find the common idea. When you find more than one with a common idea, put them into a grouping. These groups will become the major headings of your outline.

An orphan note card is one that doesn't seem to fit into any group. Orphan cards cause special problems for your outline. If you think that the information is important enough to use in your report, you might have to do more research to find supporting information. If you don't feel that your orphan is important, set it aside or even throw it out!

When you have identified the groups, you'll need to decide just what the common thread is that runs through each group. Write this common heading at the top of the index cards.

There are two types of helicopters.

A single-rotor helicopter has one main rotor above its body. A twin-rotor helicopter has two main rotors. The twin rotors move in opposite directions.

Helicopters fly because of lift.

Lift causes the helicopter to stay in the air. The special shape of the blades helps give lift. Pilots control lift by changing the angle of the blades. The engine turns the rotor and the blades cause it to lift.

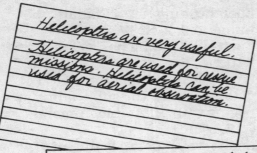

Helicopters are very useful.

Helicopters are used for rescue missions. Helicopters can be used for aerial observation.

This doesn't seem to belong.

The heaviest helicopter ever made was a 28-metric-ton Russian Mil Mi-26.

OUTLINE STRUCTURES

Outlines follow a specific pattern of headings and subheadings. The headings make general statements. The sub-headings are related to the headings and add detail to the general idea.

Your topic sentence goes at the top of your outline. Your whole outline should relate to the topic sentence. Outlines follow these general rules:

1. Each heading has a Roman numeral (I, II, III, IV, V, etc.).
2. Each subheading has a capital letter (A, B, C, etc.).
3. If you need to add a third level of detail beneath the subheading, it begins with an Arabic numeral (1, 2, 3, etc.).
4. Each level of detail is indented.

The basic pattern goes like this:
Topic sentence
   I. Heading
      A. Subheading
        1. More detail
      B. Subheading
  II. Heading
      A. Subheading
      B. Subheading
      C. Subheading
 III. Heading
      A. Subheading
      B. Subheading

✔ ADDING FLESH TO YOUR OUTLINE

There are several ways to flesh out the skeleton of your outline.

☐ **Sentence outline.** A sentence outline uses complete sentences for its headings and subheadings. Some teachers prefer this type of outline because it forces you to think in complete thoughts. A big advantage of this type of outline is that you can use your headings as the first sentence of each paragraph in your written report!

☐ **Topic outline.** A topic outline just uses words and phrases to describe the content. This type of outline isn't as detailed as a sentence outline. It leaves more to your imagination. These outlines are easier to make, but you may have a harder time using one of them later to actually write your paper.

☐**Combination outline.** A combination outline uses complete sentences for its headings and words or phrases for its subheadings.

FITTING YOUR NOTES INTO AN OUTLINE

Grouping your cards revealed the major divisions of your information. Your next step is to study these groupings and decide the order in which they should appear in your outline.

Outlines can be organized in many ways. Three of the most popular kinds are:

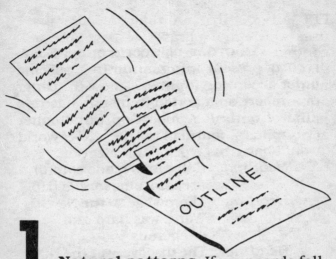

1 **Natural patterns.** If your cards fall into a logical pattern of related headings, this is the type of outline you will use. These divisions flow logically from one thought to the next. This is the most popular kind of outline organization. The note cards for the helicopter report showed this natural pattern of division.

Heading: Helicopters fly because of lift.

Heading: There are two types of helicopters.

Heading: Helicopters are very useful.

2 **In order of occurrence.** Some reports present information in a specific order according to time. A "how-to" paper or a report on a period in history has this kind of outline. A report on Christopher Columbus's journey to the New World would have this type of organization.

Heading: Columbus made careful preparations for his trip.

Heading: The voyage to the New World was hard and dangerous.

Heading: The discovery of the New World was a surprise.

It would be weird to write this report in any other order. You wouldn't talk about the preparations after telling how Columbus had already discovered the New World!

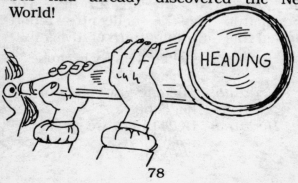

3 **Most or least important.** Some topics may be appropriate for the type of organization that gives details in degrees of importance. A report on "Land Purchases in American History" could be outlined with headings from the most important to least important like this:

Heading: The Louisiana Purchase added part or all of 15 states.

Heading: The Alaska Purchase added nearly 600,000 square miles to the U.S.

Heading: The Gadsden Purchase added parts of New Mexico and Arizona to the U.S.

You can also reverse this process. You can use the type of outline that builds from the least important to the most important. These papers build up to a big conclusion.

LEAST IMPORTANT

MOST IMPORTANT

THE FINISHED PRODUCT

Arrange your note cards in the same order as your outline. In one of the corners of each card, write the number of the heading and the letter of the subheading that matches each card to the outline.

Let's see how all this information pays off in a finished outline.

Topic Sentence and Outline

A helicopter is a type of flying machine which is lifted into the air by rotating blades.

I. Helicopters fly because lift keeps them in the air.

  A. The special shape of the blades help give lift.

  B. The engine turns the rotor and the blades generate lift.

  C. Pilots control lift by changing the angle of the blades.

II. There are two types of helicopters.

  A. A single-rotor helicopter has

one main rotor mounted above
its body.
B. A twin-rotor helicopter has
two main rotors.
1. The rotors turn in opposite
directions.
III. The helicopter is very useful.
A. Helicopters are used for rescue
missions.
B. Helicopters are used for aerial
observations.

✓ YOU'RE OFF AND RUNNING!

At last you've reached the point where
you can get down to writing your report.
Your job will be a lot easier with a good
written outline. It's time to move on to
the next step: writing the rough draft.

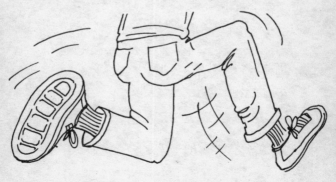

6

Writing at last: First through final drafts

At long last you can begin writing your report—almost. You don't expect to turn out a polished paper without a little practice, do you?

Professional writers call the practice version of their work a "rough" draft, or first draft. It is "rough" because it may have errors in spelling, punctuation, and grammar. The first draft will not have the smoothness you expect of a finished paper. The sentences may be choppy, and your word choices may not be "just right."

You will have a chance to smooth out the roughness of this version in the final draft. Your job in this first draft is to write down all the information which you have gathered. In your final draft you will be able to make changes and improvements.

ROUGH
DRAFT

FINAL
DRAFT

FIRST DRAFT FORMAT

Your outline and note cards are the tools you will use to build your first draft. As you use them, follow these simple rules to get started:

☐ **Double-space.** The first draft, whether it is handwritten or typed, should always be double-spaced. You might even want to use triple-spacing to give yourself more room for the changes you will make to your paper.

☐ **Write on one side of the paper.** Never write on the back of your papers. You may want to spread all of your pages out at some point so that you can see the entire picture.

☐ **Use wide margins.** Use at least one-inch margins on both sides of your page. When you begin working to improve your rough version, you may need the extra room to write in changes.

☐ **Don't worry about the length.** Write your first draft without thinking about how long it should be. Your first version may be too short or too long. You can expand it or shorten it later.

EXPAND

OR

SHORTEN

✓ READY, SET—START WRITING!

Do you feel as if you have just been thrown into shark-infested waters? Are you wondering where to start now that you are finally at the beginning?

Relax. You have everything you need to write your report right in front of you.

Read your outline again. Examine your note cards for details one at a time. Now, take a deep breath, pick up your pen, and start writing.

Start with your topic sentence on the top line. Then follow your outline carefully from point to point. Make a separate paragraph for each heading. Be sure to fill in the details from your note cards.

Keep these tips in mind:

□ **Begin anywhere.** If you get stuck writing one part of your report, move on to another section. The outline structure allows you to write each part separately. Each section in your paper should be able to stand alone. Then you can pull together all the separate parts in the final draft.

□ **Don't worry.** Let your writing come naturally. Don't think you have to use fancy words and make everything perfect. If the words aren't right, you can fix them later.

□ **Use your own words.** Resist any last-minute temptation to copy your report from an encyclopedia or some other source! See, you just don't need to. Plus your teacher knows all those tricks, so why not give him a treat by carefully putting your information into your own words?

Do your own thing!

TAKE A BREAK!

Once you've written your rough draft, you need to take a break. Put your report aside and forget about it for a little while.

If you've been using your time wisely, you should be able to take a break from your report for a few days. If your paper is due tomorrow, at least stop long enough to get a snack.

This "cool-down" period is an important step. After a short break, you can look at your report through fresh eyes. This helps you see any of the paper's weaknesses. When you've been working on a report for a long time, it is hard to see problems that may be hiding in the paper.

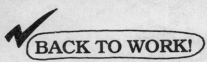

BACK TO WORK!

Whether your break was one hour or one week, you must eventually get back to the paper to finish it up. When you read your rough draft again, pretend you are grading it. Take a red pen and mark mistakes you made or changes you'd like to make right on the paper.

Your rough draft is a "working" paper. If your teacher wants you to turn in this draft, she won't expect it to look good. Make your changes in the margins and between your double-spaced lines.

Be sure to do these things when revising your draft:

☐ **Check for style.** Check for spelling and punctuation errors. Make sure you've used complete sentences. Does every sentence have a subject and a verb? Does each sentence express a complete thought? Did you accidentally switch from one verb tense to another?

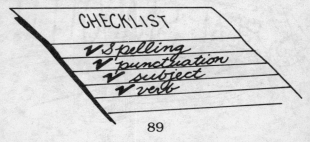

☐ **Check the structure.** Did you stick to the point? Did you say what you meant to say? Double-check your outline and note cards. Did you leave out any important information? Did you include unnecessary information? Do the sentences flow together? Is each of the paragraphs connected to the topic sentence?

How Does It Sound?

Try reading your report out loud. Listen carefully to make sure that each section flows smoothly into the next. Does it sound choppy? Reading your report out loud will help you "hear" it the way your teacher will.

✓ GET A SECOND OPINION

If your doctor told you that you needed an operation, you might go to another doctor to get a second opinion. You may think that your report is fine now, but other people may disagree. It makes sense to get a second opinion.

Ask your parents or some other adult to read your paper. Ask the adult to look out for errors in grammar, punctuation, and spelling, as well as for problems with the organization of the paper.

Take his or her comments seriously and make the necessary changes to your rough draft.

✔ THE FINAL DRAFT

Your final draft is the version that contains all of the corrections and changes you've made to your report. It is the polished form of your rough draft.

If it's okay with your teacher, use an erasable pen to write your final draft. Mistakes in copying *do* creep in, and with this kind of pen you won't have to rewrite a whole page. Leave ample margins (sides and bottom) in case you need to slip in an extra word that you left out.

When you are satisfied that your report is now the best that you can make it, turn back to the Teacher-Pleasing Paper Planner in Chapter 1. Make sure that your paper meets all the standards your teacher has set. Don't spoil a great written report simply by failing to present it in the form that your teacher requires.

Your finished report consists of several different parts. Put them together in this order:

1 **Cover or title page.** The cover or title page is the first page of your report. Your teacher may give you specific directions on how to arrange the cover page information. All cover pages should include the title of the report, your name, and the date.

2 **The report.** The final draft of your report is directly behind the cover page.

3 **Extras.** If your teacher requires any supporting material, such as maps, charts, or pictures, put them behind the text of your report.

4 **Bibliography.** Make sure that your bibliography page includes all the resources you have used for your report. The bibliography is the last page of your report.

WRAPPING IT ALL UP

Take one last look at your report to make sure that you haven't left anything out. Be sure that your name is on the front of the report. You might even want to put your name on each page. And make sure the pages are numbered. Then put the report in a folder and staple it together.

Now, turn it in and relax. Your good grade is assured.

Congratulations! By following the eight basic steps for writing reports, you've ended up with your best report ever! You really *can* do it!

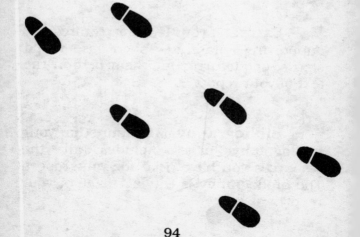

94

For your
great work
you deserve
a gift!

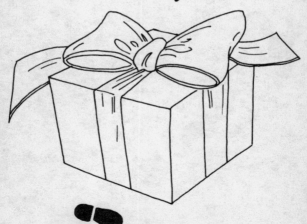